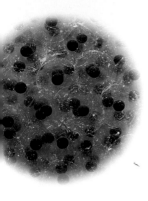

KU-330-687

Contents

The frog in this book is the common frog, which lives in Europe and Asia. Panels at the top of the pages show when each stage in the frog's life cycle takes place. The sections on a yellow background give information about the life cycles of other amphibians as well as other frog species.

Words in **bold** are explained in the glossary on page 30.

Time panel

Information about other amphibians and frog species

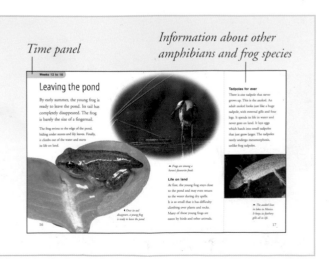

What is a frog?

Frogs are small animals with four legs that live in and around ponds. Frogs are **amphibians**. These are animals that can live both in water and on land. Toads and newts are also amphibians.

Jumping and swimming

Frogs have powerful back legs that are ideal for jumping. When a frog is in water, it uses its back legs for swimming. Frogs have a moist skin which loses water easily. This means that they prefer to live in damp places near water.

They have **lungs** for breathing, but because these are weak, frogs have to breathe through their skin as well.

▶ *The common frog is an amphibian with four legs and moist skin.*

4

▲ *When a frog is in water, it uses its long back legs for swimming.*

From egg to adult

Frogs spend their adult life on land, living in grass and under **shrubs**. But they have to return to the water to **breed**. Adult female frogs lay their eggs in a pond or a stream.

The eggs hatch into young animals called **tadpoles**. The tadpoles have to go through a complete change in shape and appearance to become adults. This change is called **metamorphosis**.

Laying eggs

In spring, frogs make their way from their winter hiding places to the ponds and slow-flowing streams where they breed. Sometimes they make journeys of several kilometres.

Croaking frogs

The male frogs usually reach the pond first, where they wait for the females to arrive. The males croak loudly to attract the attention of the female frogs. They do this by forcing air through a **voice box** in their throats. The croaks sound particularly loud at night.

◀ *A common frog blows out the pouches on the sides of its throat to make its croaks even louder.*

Mating

The frogs **mate** in the pond. The female frogs are fat with eggs. A male climbs on to a female's back, places his front legs around her chest and grips her tightly. Sometimes, frogs stay like this for several days.

The female starts to lay her eggs, and at the same time the male releases **sperm** which **fertilizes** the eggs. Each female frog lays a clump of about 100 eggs, but not all the eggs will hatch. The clumps of eggs are called **frogspawn**.

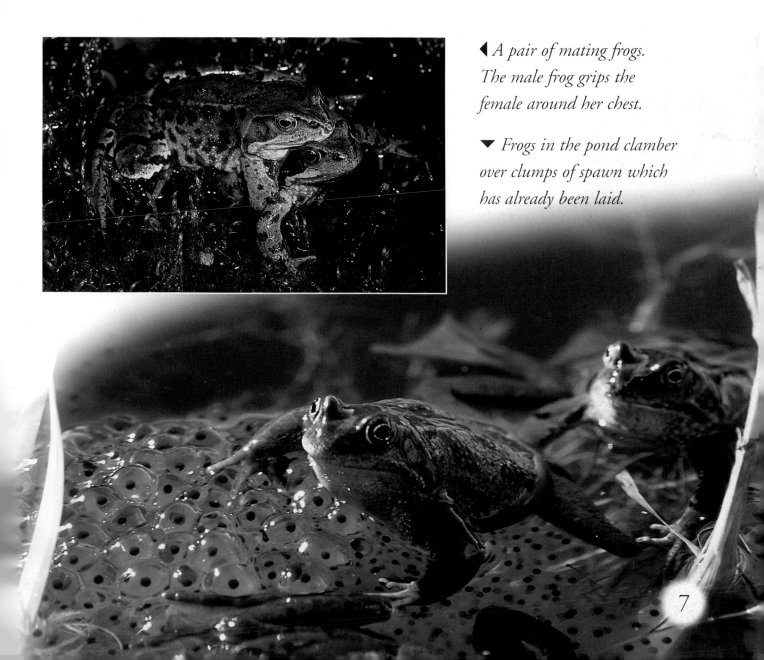

◀ *A pair of mating frogs. The male frog grips the female around her chest.*

▼ *Frogs in the pond clamber over clumps of spawn which has already been laid.*

Inside a frog's egg

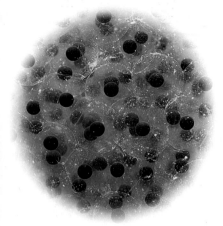

▲ *A clump of newly-laid spawn.*

A newly-laid egg is a tiny black dot in the middle of a blob of clear jelly. Hundreds of eggs stick together to form a wobbly mass that floats on the surface of the pond.

The black dot is made up of a single **cell** and a store of food called the **yolk**. The yolk will be the source of food for the tadpole during its first few weeks of life. At first the eggs are small. But the jelly **absorbs** water and swells in size. After two or three days, the frogspawn has grown many times larger.

Slippery eggs

The jelly sticks the eggs together and stops them from drying out. It is almost impossible to separate them. Because the jelly is slippery too, animals find the eggs difficult to grip. This protects them from being eaten.

▶ *The jelly may stick to plants in the water, which stops the eggs being swept away.*

▲ *Mating toads have laid long chains of toadspawn in this pond.*

Chains of eggs

Toads lay their eggs in long chains that wrap around pond plants. Each chain looks like a row of black dots. Newts lay their eggs one by one on the leaves of pond plants.

▼ *This newt will take several days to lay her eggs.*

From egg to tadpole

The eggs start growing straight away. The single cell that forms an egg divides to form two cells. The two cells divide to form four cells, which divide again to make eight cells, and so on. Before long, there is a ball of cells.

After two days, the black ball begins to change shape and become longer. Soon, you can see a tiny tadpole. The tadpole grows larger, but it is still protected inside the blob of jelly.

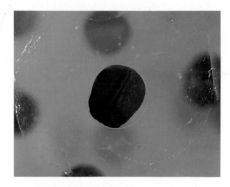

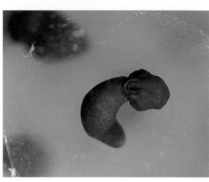

▲ *After a few days, the black ball (top) changes into a tiny tadpole (bottom).*

▼ *After ten days, a tadpole can move in its jelly.*

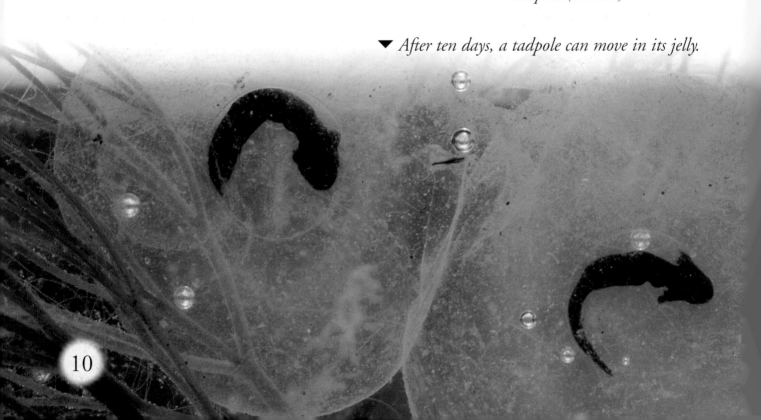

▲ *At first, newly-hatched tadpoles stay close to other eggs.*

Hatching

After ten days, the jelly around the tadpole turns to liquid, so the tadpole can move around. Then the tadpole wriggles its way out of the jelly and into the water. Its mouth has not opened, and it is still very small. Its **abdomen** is swollen with the remains of the yolk. This provides the tadpole with food until it can feed itself. For the next few days, the tadpole stays close to the jelly or clings to nearby pondweed. Then its mouth opens and it swims away into the pond.

Foam nests

Not all frogs lay their eggs in a pond. Some tree frogs in the **tropics** lay eggs inside a foam nest on a leaf. The tadpoles hatch and begin to grow inside the nest. Then they drop off the leaf into a pond below.

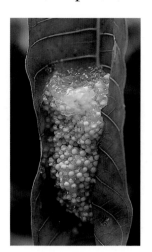

◀ *A foam nest on a leaf in the rainforest.*

String of eggs

The male midwife toad carries a string of eggs around its back legs. After a few weeks, the eggs hatch into well-developed tadpoles.

▼ *A male midwife toad with its eggs.*

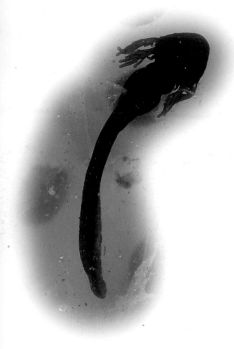

Tadpoles

For the first few days after it hatches, the tadpole clings to the eggs or to pondweed with its tail hanging down. It has tiny feathery **gills** on each side of its head. The tadpole breathes by taking in **oxygen** from the water through its gills.

▼ *These young tadpoles are clinging to a mass of eggs.*

▶ After four weeks, the external gills have been replaced by internal gills.

Growing fast

Young tadpoles are plant-eaters, or **herbivores**. They grow larger and stronger by feeding on pondweed and tiny **algae** in the water. This is when the tadpoles grow fastest. Their long tails help them to swim further and further. The tadpoles gather near the surface of the water and around the edge of the pond, where the water is shallow and warm.

In danger

At first there are hundreds of tadpoles in the pond, but as the weeks pass there are fewer swimming around. They are eaten by other pond animals, such as backswimmers, diving beetles and dragonfly **larvae**.

Disappearing gills

The gills outside a tadpole's body – called external gills – soon start to grow smaller. After four weeks, they have disappeared. They are replaced by internal gills, which are protected on the outside by a flap of skin.

*▼ This dragonfly larva is a **predator**. It feeds on young tadpoles.*

13

Growing legs

When a tadpole is about eight weeks old, it starts to change into a frog. Two small bulges appear at the back of its body, on either side of the tail.

Legs and feet

The bulges are the first sign that the tadpole's back legs are starting to grow. The bulges quickly develop into legs. Each leg ends in a webbed foot. The front legs appear a few weeks later. By now the tadpole is eating small plants such as duckweed, and **microscopic** animals in the water.

1 *The back legs appear first, after about eight weeks.*

2 *The tadpole's body starts to change shape as its back legs grow larger.*

3 *The front legs appear a few weeks later. This tadpole is taking its first gulp of air.*

Changes inside

Inside the tadpole's body, its lungs grow and slowly take over from the internal gills. Now the tadpole comes to the surface of the water to gulp air. The **gut** gets shorter as the tadpole changes from a plant to a meat diet.

Disappearing tail

The tadpole is still changing shape. Its body slowly absorbs the tail, which grows shorter and shorter until just a stump remains. The **backbone** becomes more obvious. The round mouth of the tadpole changes to the much wider mouth of the frog, and its eyes become more **bulbous**.

▼ *This young frog still has the stump of its tail.*

Leaving the pond

By early summer, the young frog is ready to leave the pond. Its tail has completely disappeared. The frog is barely the size of a fingernail.

The frog swims to the edge of the pond, hiding under stones and lily leaves. Finally, it climbs out of the water and starts its life on land.

◀ *Once its tail disappears, a young frog is ready to leave the pond.*

Tadpoles forever

There is one tadpole that never grows up. This is the axolotl. An adult axolotl looks just like a huge tadpole, with external gills and four legs. It spends its life in water and never goes on land. It lays eggs which hatch into small tadpoles that just grow larger. The tadpoles rarely go through metamorphosis, unlike frog tadpoles.

▲ *Frogs are among a heron's favourite foods.*

Life on land

At first, the young frog stays close to the pond and may even return to the water during dry spells. It is so small that it has difficulty climbing over plants and rocks. Many of these young frogs are eaten by birds and other animals.

▲ *The axolotl lives in lakes in Mexico. It keeps its feathery gills all its life.*

Hunting and jumping

A young frog has to learn how to find food. Frog tadpoles are herbivores, but an adult frog is a **carnivore**, or meat-eater. It eats small animals such as flies and other insects.

▲ *A frog's large eyes can see well by day and by night.*

Sticky tongues

A frog has a long, sticky tongue which is attached to the front of its mouth and points backwards. When an insect flies past, the frog flicks out its tongue to catch it. The insect is whisked into the frog's mouth and swallowed.

The eyes of a frog are large and bulge out from the top of its head. They are very sensitive to movement. A frog probably won't see another animal if it remains perfectly still, but will spot it as soon as it moves.

▶ *A frog can flick out its tongue and catch its prey in a fraction of a second.*

Powerful legs

Frogs are very good at jumping. The powerful muscles in a frog's back legs push it forwards at great speed. The back legs are great for swimming, too. There are flaps of skin between the toes. These webbed feet act like flippers or paddles, pushing the frog through the water.

▶ *Powerful back legs and webbed feet are ideal for swimming.*

▼ *On land, a frog uses its back legs for hopping and leaping.*

Surviving winter

A young frog grows quickly during its first summer. It has to build up food stores in its body which will help it survive cold winter weather.

▲ *This frog has found a hole where it can spend the winter.*

Warm or cold?

The body temperature of a frog is the same temperature as the frog's surroundings, or environment. When it is warm, the frog's body is warm. But in cold weather, its body temperature falls. The scientific word for this is **ectothermic**. Humans are different – our body temperature stays the same, whatever the temperature is outside.

Winter sleep

In winter, the weather is too cold for frogs. They would not be able to find food, so they **hibernate**, or go into a deep sleep. As winter approaches, a frog finds a safe place to hibernate – under logs or at the bottom of a pond, for example. It stays there until spring arrives and the temperature rises.

◀ *Frogs may spend the winter hidden under logs, where the temperature will stay above freezing.*

▲ *In the desert, burrowing frogs appear above ground as soon as rain falls, ready to breed.*

Underground burrows

Sometimes, the weather is too hot and dry for frogs. In the desert, burrowing frogs survive the hot weather by burying themselves underground. They stay in their cool burrows until the rains arrive. Then they emerge and lay eggs in ponds and puddles. The tadpoles have to complete their metamorphosis before the ponds dry up.

Back to the pond

▲ A fully-grown frog has a body up to 10 cm long.

A frog takes about two or three years to reach full size. The first years of its life are spent eating and growing. By the third year, it is fully **mature** and ready to breed.

A dangerous journey

In spring, frogs go back to the pond where they were born. Longer hours of daylight and rising temperatures tell them when it is time to start their journey. Frogs find their way back by recognizing landmarks. Some even use the position of the sun and stars.

The journey can be dangerous. A frog may have to cross roads and could be run over. It may find that the pond has dried up, or been filled in and the land used for building. Once a female frog reaches the pond, it finds a mate and begins egg-laying.

▲ Many frogs and toads are killed by traffic as they return to ponds in spring.

Frogs crossing!

Near some ponds in spring, road signs warn drivers that there may be frogs or toads on the road ahead.

▼ This frog is returning to the pond where it was born.

Sometimes, so many frogs and toads cross the road that people stay beside the road all night, picking up the animals and carrying them to safety.

Growing old

Frogs can live for 25 years or more in **captivity**. In the wild, frogs more than a few years old are rare. Many are eaten by birds such as herons and egrets. Foxes, snakes and hedgehogs eat frogs, too.

▲ *You are more likely to see old frogs in town gardens, where there are fewer predators.*

A dangerous life

Frogs also die from diseases and **parasites** – tiny animals that live on or inside the frog. Frogs can be killed by **polluted** water and by **pesticides** that run into ponds and streams from fields and gardens. Pesticides also kill the insects that frogs like to eat.

◀ *Frogs and tadpoles are easily harmed by polluted water. They either die or move away.*

Defensive action

When toads are attacked, they defend themselves by standing up on their legs and **inflating** their bodies with air. This makes them look much bigger than they really are. They also give off a foul-tasting, **poisonous** white substance through their skin. Some amphibians have brightly-coloured bodies, which are a warning to predators that they are poisonous.

▶ *This tree frog has been caught by a snake in the rainforest.*

▼ *The yellowy-orange underside of the fire-bellied toad is a warning to predators to stay away.*

All sorts of amphibians

There are about 3500 different types of amphibians. Most of them are frogs or toads.

◀ *This common toad has shorter legs than a common frog. Its body is more rounded, with dry and lumpy skin.*

Frog or toad?

How can you tell the difference between a frog and a toad? A frog has smooth, moist skin. The skin of a toad is lumpy and much drier.

A frog is usually slimmer than a toad and its legs tend to be longer. Both animals have a short back and no tail.

◀ *This green tree frog has smooth, moist skin and long back legs.*

Newts and salamanders

Newts and salamanders look like lizards, with long bodies and an even longer tail. But they have moist skin, while lizards have dry, scaly skin. Newts and salamanders move slowly and cannot hop or jump.

When newts mate, the male dances in front of the female. The eggs hatch into tadpoles that look like those of the frog. Although each tadpole grows legs, its tail does not change.

◀ *The salamander looks like a lizard, but it has moist skin.*

▼ *Newts leave the water at the end of the breeding season to live on land. They hunt slugs and worms at night.*

Amazing amphibians

- The female African clawed toad lays up to 15 000 eggs at a time.

- The biggest frog in the world is the rare goliath frog from West Africa. Some female goliath frogs grow up to 34 cm long, and can weigh up to 3.3 kg.

- The most poisonous frog is the poison-arrow frog of South America (below). Touching it can kill you, because it gives off a poison through its skin. Its bright colours are a warning not to touch it.

- The largest toad is the cane toad of Australia (right). It can weigh up to 450g. So many cane toads live in Australia that many people think they are a **pest**.

- The world's largest amphibian is the giant salamander. It can reach lengths of 1.8m and weigh as much as 65 kg.

- The longest jumper is the South African sharp-nosed frog. It covers more than 3m in a single leap – that's 60 times its body length. If humans could do the same, we would be able to leap more than 100m.

The life cycle of a frog

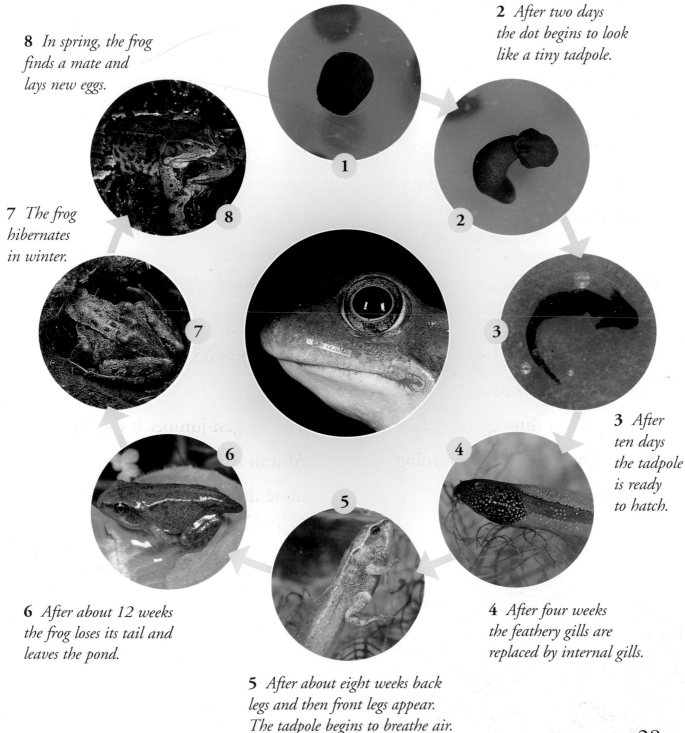

1 *A newly-laid egg is a black dot in clear jelly.*

2 *After two days the dot begins to look like a tiny tadpole.*

8 *In spring, the frog finds a mate and lays new eggs.*

7 *The frog hibernates in winter.*

3 *After ten days the tadpole is ready to hatch.*

6 *After about 12 weeks the frog loses its tail and leaves the pond.*

4 *After four weeks the feathery gills are replaced by internal gills.*

5 *After about eight weeks back legs and then front legs appear. The tadpole begins to breathe air.*

29

Glossary

abdomen The rear part of an animal.

absorb To take in or swallow up.

algae Tiny green plants that live in water. They do not have leaves, roots or flowers.

amphibian An animal with a bony skeleton and a backbone which lays jelly-covered eggs that hatch into tadpoles. All frogs, toads, newts and salamanders are amphibians.

backbone The column of bones in an animal's back.

breed To produce young.

bulbous Round and fat.

captivity An animal in captivity is one that is kept in a zoo or as a pet.

carnivore An animal that eats other animals.

cell One of the tiny building blocks that make up a living organism.

ectothermic Having a body temperature that changes with the temperature of the environment.

fertilize To join a male sperm with a female egg to form a new life.

frogspawn The name given to a mass of eggs laid by a frog.

gill The part of a fish or amphibian that absorbs oxygen from water, so that the animal can breathe underwater.

gut The digestive tube of an animal.

herbivore An animal that eats only plants.

hibernate To spend the winter in a deep sleep.

inflate To fill with a gas, such as air.

larva (plural **larvae**) The young form of an animal that hatches from an egg. A larva does not look much like its parent. The larva of a frog is a tadpole.

lungs Sponge-like organs that absorb oxygen from the air when an animal breathes in.

mate To pair or breed.

mature Fully grown.

metamorphosis A change in body shape or appearance, as when a tadpole changes into an adult frog.

microscopic Too small to be seen with the naked eye.

oxygen A gas in air and water that most plants and animals need to survive.

parasite An animal that lives in or on another living animal and harms it.

pest An animal that damages crops.

pesticide A chemical used to kill pests such as greenfly and locusts.

poisonous Harmful.

polluted Containing harmful or poisonous substances.

predator An animal that hunts and kills other animals for food.

shrub A small, tree-like bush.

sperm The male cell which fertilizes a female egg to create a new animal.

tadpole The young form of an amphibian, before it changes into an adult.

tropics The areas on each side of the Equator, where it is warm and wet for all or most of the year.

voice box The upper part of the windpipe, which produces sounds.

yolk The food store in an egg.

Index